Password Journal

Black Eyes

ISBN 978-1-329-19279-9

NAME:	
SITE ADDRESS:	
USERNAME:	
PASSWORD:	
NOTES:	

NAME:	
SITE ADDRESS:	
USERNAME:	
PASSWORD:	
NOTES:	

NAME:	
SITE ADDRESS:	
USERNAME:	
PASSWORD:	
NOTES:	

NAME:	
SITE ADDRESS:	
USERNAME:	
PASSWORD:	
NOTES:	

NAME:	
SITE ADDRESS:	
USERNAME:	
PASSWORD:	
NOTES:	

NAME:	
SITE ADDRESS:	
USERNAME:	
PASSWORD:	
NOTES:	

NAME:	
SITE ADDRESS:	
USERNAME:	
PASSWORD:	
NOTES:	

NAME:	
SITE ADDRESS:	
USERNAME:	
PASSWORD:	
NOTES:	

NAME:	
SITE ADDRESS:	
USERNAME:	
PASSWORD:	
NOTES:	

NAME:	
SITE ADDRESS:	
USERNAME:	
PASSWORD:	
NOTES:	

NAME:	
SITE ADDRESS:	
USERNAME:	
PASSWORD:	
NOTES:	

NAME:	
SITE ADDRESS:	
USERNAME:	
PASSWORD:	
NOTES:	

NAME:	
SITE ADDRESS:	
USERNAME:	
PASSWORD:	
NOTES:	

NAME:	
SITE ADDRESS:	
USERNAME:	
PASSWORD:	
NOTES:	

NAME:	
SITE ADDRESS:	
USERNAME:	
PASSWORD:	
NOTES:	

NAME:	
SITE ADDRESS:	
USERNAME:	
PASSWORD:	
NOTES:	

NAME:	
SITE ADDRESS:	
USERNAME:	
PASSWORD:	
NOTES:	

NAME:	
SITE ADDRESS:	
USERNAME:	
PASSWORD:	
NOTES:	

NAME:	
SITE ADDRESS:	
USERNAME:	
PASSWORD:	
NOTES:	

NAME:	
SITE ADDRESS:	
USERNAME:	
PASSWORD:	
NOTES:	

NAME:	
SITE ADDRESS:	
USERNAME:	
PASSWORD:	
NOTES:	

NAME:	
SITE ADDRESS:	
USERNAME:	
PASSWORD:	
NOTES:	

NAME:	
SITE ADDRESS:	
USERNAME:	
PASSWORD:	
NOTES:	

NAME:	
SITE ADDRESS:	
USERNAME:	
PASSWORD:	
NOTES:	

NAME:	
SITE ADDRESS:	
USERNAME:	
PASSWORD:	
NOTES:	

NAME:	
SITE ADDRESS:	
USERNAME:	
PASSWORD:	
NOTES:	

NAME:	
SITE ADDRESS:	
USERNAME:	
PASSWORD:	
NOTES:	

NAME:	
SITE ADDRESS:	
USERNAME:	
PASSWORD:	
NOTES:	

NAME:	
SITE ADDRESS:	
USERNAME:	
PASSWORD:	
NOTES:	

NAME:	
SITE ADDRESS:	
USERNAME:	
PASSWORD:	
NOTES:	

NAME:	
SITE ADDRESS:	
USERNAME:	
PASSWORD:	
NOTES:	

NAME:	
SITE ADDRESS:	
USERNAME:	
PASSWORD:	
NOTES:	

NAME:	
SITE ADDRESS:	
USERNAME:	
PASSWORD:	
NOTES:	

NAME:	
SITE ADDRESS:	
USERNAME:	
PASSWORD:	
NOTES:	

NAME:	
SITE ADDRESS:	
USERNAME:	
PASSWORD:	
NOTES:	

NAME:	
SITE ADDRESS:	
USERNAME:	
PASSWORD:	
NOTES:	

NAME:	
SITE ADDRESS:	
USERNAME:	
PASSWORD:	
NOTES:	

NAME:	
SITE ADDRESS:	
USERNAME:	
PASSWORD:	
NOTES:	

NAME:	
SITE ADDRESS:	
USERNAME:	
PASSWORD:	
NOTES:	

NAME:	
SITE ADDRESS:	
USERNAME:	
PASSWORD:	
NOTES:	

NAME:	
SITE ADDRESS:	
USERNAME:	
PASSWORD:	
NOTES:	

NAME:	
SITE ADDRESS:	
USERNAME:	
PASSWORD:	
NOTES:	

NAME:	
SITE ADDRESS:	
USERNAME:	
PASSWORD:	
NOTES:	

NAME:	
SITE ADDRESS:	
USERNAME:	
PASSWORD:	
NOTES:	

NAME:	
SITE ADDRESS:	
USERNAME:	
PASSWORD:	
NOTES:	

NAME:	
SITE ADDRESS:	
USERNAME:	
PASSWORD:	
NOTES:	

NAME:	
SITE ADDRESS:	
USERNAME:	
PASSWORD:	
NOTES:	

NAME:	
SITE ADDRESS:	
USERNAME:	
PASSWORD:	
NOTES:	

NAME:	
SITE ADDRESS:	
USERNAME:	
PASSWORD:	
NOTES:	

NAME:	
SITE ADDRESS:	
USERNAME:	
PASSWORD:	
NOTES:	

NAME:	
SITE ADDRESS:	
USERNAME:	
PASSWORD:	
NOTES:	

NAME:	
SITE ADDRESS:	
USERNAME:	
PASSWORD:	
NOTES:	

NAME:	
SITE ADDRESS:	
USERNAME:	
PASSWORD:	
NOTES:	

NAME:	
SITE ADDRESS:	
USERNAME:	
PASSWORD:	
NOTES:	

NAME:	
SITE ADDRESS:	
USERNAME:	
PASSWORD:	
NOTES:	

NAME:	
SITE ADDRESS:	
USERNAME:	
PASSWORD:	
NOTES:	

NAME:	
SITE ADDRESS:	
USERNAME:	
PASSWORD:	
NOTES:	

NAME:	
SITE ADDRESS:	
USERNAME:	
PASSWORD:	
NOTES:	

NAME:	
SITE ADDRESS:	
USERNAME:	
PASSWORD:	
NOTES:	

NAME:	
SITE ADDRESS:	
USERNAME:	
PASSWORD:	
NOTES:	

NAME:	
SITE ADDRESS:	
USERNAME:	
PASSWORD:	
NOTES:	

NAME:	
SITE ADDRESS:	
USERNAME:	
PASSWORD:	
NOTES:	

NAME:	
SITE ADDRESS:	
USERNAME:	
PASSWORD:	
NOTES:	

NAME:	
SITE ADDRESS:	
USERNAME:	
PASSWORD:	
NOTES:	

NAME:	
SITE ADDRESS:	
USERNAME:	
PASSWORD:	
NOTES:	

NAME:	
SITE ADDRESS:	
USERNAME:	
PASSWORD:	
NOTES:	

NAME:	
SITE ADDRESS:	
USERNAME:	
PASSWORD:	
NOTES:	

NAME:	
SITE ADDRESS:	
USERNAME:	
PASSWORD:	
NOTES:	

NAME:	
SITE ADDRESS:	
USERNAME:	
PASSWORD:	
NOTES:	

NAME:	
SITE ADDRESS:	
USERNAME:	
PASSWORD:	
NOTES:	

NAME:	
SITE ADDRESS:	
USERNAME:	
PASSWORD:	
NOTES:	

NAME:	
SITE ADDRESS:	
USERNAME:	
PASSWORD:	
NOTES:	

NAME:	
SITE ADDRESS:	
USERNAME:	
PASSWORD:	
NOTES:	

NAME:	
SITE ADDRESS:	
USERNAME:	
PASSWORD:	
NOTES:	

NAME:	
SITE ADDRESS:	
USERNAME:	
PASSWORD:	
NOTES:	

NAME:	
SITE ADDRESS:	
USERNAME:	
PASSWORD:	
NOTES:	

NAME:	
SITE ADDRESS:	
USERNAME:	
PASSWORD:	
NOTES:	

NAME:	
SITE ADDRESS:	
USERNAME:	
PASSWORD:	
NOTES:	

NAME:	
SITE ADDRESS:	
USERNAME:	
PASSWORD:	
NOTES:	

NAME:	
SITE ADDRESS:	
USERNAME:	
PASSWORD:	
NOTES:	

NAME:	
SITE ADDRESS:	
USERNAME:	
PASSWORD:	
NOTES:	

NAME:	
SITE ADDRESS:	
USERNAME:	
PASSWORD:	
NOTES:	

NAME:	
SITE ADDRESS:	
USERNAME:	
PASSWORD:	
NOTES:	

NAME:	
SITE ADDRESS:	
USERNAME:	
PASSWORD:	
NOTES:	

NAME:	
SITE ADDRESS:	
USERNAME:	
PASSWORD:	
NOTES:	

NAME:	
SITE ADDRESS:	
USERNAME:	
PASSWORD:	
NOTES:	

NAME:	
SITE ADDRESS:	
USERNAME:	
PASSWORD:	
NOTES:	

NAME:	
SITE ADDRESS:	
USERNAME:	
PASSWORD:	
NOTES:	

NAME:	
SITE ADDRESS:	
USERNAME:	
PASSWORD:	
NOTES:	

NAME:	
SITE ADDRESS:	
USERNAME:	
PASSWORD:	
NOTES:	

NAME:	
SITE ADDRESS:	
USERNAME:	
PASSWORD:	
NOTES:	

NAME:	
SITE ADDRESS:	
USERNAME:	
PASSWORD:	
NOTES:	

NAME:	
SITE ADDRESS:	
USERNAME:	
PASSWORD:	
NOTES:	

NAME:	
SITE ADDRESS:	
USERNAME:	
PASSWORD:	
NOTES:	

NAME:	
SITE ADDRESS:	
USERNAME:	
PASSWORD:	
NOTES:	

NAME:	
SITE ADDRESS:	
USERNAME:	
PASSWORD:	
NOTES:	

NAME:	
SITE ADDRESS:	
USERNAME:	
PASSWORD:	
NOTES:	

NAME:	
SITE ADDRESS:	
USERNAME:	
PASSWORD:	
NOTES:	

NAME:	
SITE ADDRESS:	
USERNAME:	
PASSWORD:	
NOTES:	

NAME:	
SITE ADDRESS:	
USERNAME:	
PASSWORD:	
NOTES:	

NAME:	
SITE ADDRESS:	
USERNAME:	
PASSWORD:	
NOTES:	

NAME:	
SITE ADDRESS:	
USERNAME:	
PASSWORD:	
NOTES:	

NAME:	
SITE ADDRESS:	
USERNAME:	
PASSWORD:	
NOTES:	

NAME:	
SITE ADDRESS:	
USERNAME:	
PASSWORD:	
NOTES:	

NAME:	
SITE ADDRESS:	
USERNAME:	
PASSWORD:	
NOTES:	

NAME:	
SITE ADDRESS:	
USERNAME:	
PASSWORD:	
NOTES:	

NAME:	
SITE ADDRESS:	
USERNAME:	
PASSWORD:	
NOTES:	

NAME:	
SITE ADDRESS:	
USERNAME:	
PASSWORD:	
NOTES:	

NAME:	
SITE ADDRESS:	
USERNAME:	
PASSWORD:	
NOTES:	

NAME:	
SITE ADDRESS:	
USERNAME:	
PASSWORD:	
NOTES:	

NAME:	
SITE ADDRESS:	
USERNAME:	
PASSWORD:	
NOTES:	

NAME:	
SITE ADDRESS:	
USERNAME:	
PASSWORD:	
NOTES:	

NAME:	
SITE ADDRESS:	
USERNAME:	
PASSWORD:	
NOTES:	

NAME:	
SITE ADDRESS:	
USERNAME:	
PASSWORD:	
NOTES:	

NAME:	
SITE ADDRESS:	
USERNAME:	
PASSWORD:	
NOTES:	

NAME:	
SITE ADDRESS:	
USERNAME:	
PASSWORD:	
NOTES:	

NAME:	
SITE ADDRESS:	
USERNAME:	
PASSWORD:	
NOTES:	

NAME:	
SITE ADDRESS:	
USERNAME:	
PASSWORD:	
NOTES:	

NAME:	
SITE ADDRESS:	
USERNAME:	
PASSWORD:	
NOTES:	

NAME:	
SITE ADDRESS:	
USERNAME:	
PASSWORD:	
NOTES:	

NAME:	
SITE ADDRESS:	
USERNAME:	
PASSWORD:	
NOTES:	

NAME:	
SITE ADDRESS:	
USERNAME:	
PASSWORD:	
NOTES:	

NAME:	
SITE ADDRESS:	
USERNAME:	
PASSWORD:	
NOTES:	

NAME:	
SITE ADDRESS:	
USERNAME:	
PASSWORD:	
NOTES:	

NAME:	
SITE ADDRESS:	
USERNAME:	
PASSWORD:	
NOTES:	

NAME:	
SITE ADDRESS:	
USERNAME:	
PASSWORD:	
NOTES:	

NAME:	
SITE ADDRESS:	
USERNAME:	
PASSWORD:	
NOTES:	

NAME:	
SITE ADDRESS:	
USERNAME:	
PASSWORD:	
NOTES:	

NAME:	
SITE ADDRESS:	
USERNAME:	
PASSWORD:	
NOTES:	

NAME:	
SITE ADDRESS:	
USERNAME:	
PASSWORD:	
NOTES:	

NAME:	
SITE ADDRESS:	
USERNAME:	
PASSWORD:	
NOTES:	

NAME:	
SITE ADDRESS:	
USERNAME:	
PASSWORD:	
NOTES:	

NAME:	
SITE ADDRESS:	
USERNAME:	
PASSWORD:	
NOTES:	

NAME:	
SITE ADDRESS:	
USERNAME:	
PASSWORD:	
NOTES:	

NAME:	
SITE ADDRESS:	
USERNAME:	
PASSWORD:	
NOTES:	

NAME:	
SITE ADDRESS:	
USERNAME:	
PASSWORD:	
NOTES:	

NAME:	
SITE ADDRESS:	
USERNAME:	
PASSWORD:	
NOTES:	

NAME:	
SITE ADDRESS:	
USERNAME:	
PASSWORD:	
NOTES:	

NAME:	
SITE ADDRESS:	
USERNAME:	
PASSWORD:	
NOTES:	

NAME:	
SITE ADDRESS:	
USERNAME:	
PASSWORD:	
NOTES:	

NAME:	
SITE ADDRESS:	
USERNAME:	
PASSWORD:	
NOTES:	

NAME:	
SITE ADDRESS:	
USERNAME:	
PASSWORD:	
NOTES:	

NAME:	
SITE ADDRESS:	
USERNAME:	
PASSWORD:	
NOTES:	

NAME:	
SITE ADDRESS:	
USERNAME:	
PASSWORD:	
NOTES:	

NAME:	
SITE ADDRESS:	
USERNAME:	
PASSWORD:	
NOTES:	

NAME:	
SITE ADDRESS:	
USERNAME:	
PASSWORD:	
NOTES:	

NAME:	
SITE ADDRESS:	
USERNAME:	
PASSWORD:	
NOTES:	

NAME:	
SITE ADDRESS:	
USERNAME:	
PASSWORD:	
NOTES:	

NAME:	
SITE ADDRESS:	
USERNAME:	
PASSWORD:	
NOTES:	

NAME:	
SITE ADDRESS:	
USERNAME:	
PASSWORD:	
NOTES:	

NAME:	
SITE ADDRESS:	
USERNAME:	
PASSWORD:	
NOTES:	

NAME:	
SITE ADDRESS:	
USERNAME:	
PASSWORD:	
NOTES:	

NAME:	
SITE ADDRESS:	
USERNAME:	
PASSWORD:	
NOTES:	

NAME:	
SITE ADDRESS:	
USERNAME:	
PASSWORD:	
NOTES:	

NAME:	
SITE ADDRESS:	
USERNAME:	
PASSWORD:	
NOTES:	

NAME:	
SITE ADDRESS:	
USERNAME:	
PASSWORD:	
NOTES:	

NAME:	
SITE ADDRESS:	
USERNAME:	
PASSWORD:	
NOTES:	

NAME:	
SITE ADDRESS:	
USERNAME:	
PASSWORD:	
NOTES:	

NAME:	
SITE ADDRESS:	
USERNAME:	
PASSWORD:	
NOTES:	

NAME:	
SITE ADDRESS:	
USERNAME:	
PASSWORD:	
NOTES:	

NAME:	
SITE ADDRESS:	
USERNAME:	
PASSWORD:	
NOTES:	

NAME:	
SITE ADDRESS:	
USERNAME:	
PASSWORD:	
NOTES:	

NAME:	
SITE ADDRESS:	
USERNAME:	
PASSWORD:	
NOTES:	

NAME:	
SITE ADDRESS:	
USERNAME:	
PASSWORD:	
NOTES:	

NAME:	
SITE ADDRESS:	
USERNAME:	
PASSWORD:	
NOTES:	

NAME:	
SITE ADDRESS:	
USERNAME:	
PASSWORD:	
NOTES:	

NAME:	
SITE ADDRESS:	
USERNAME:	
PASSWORD:	
NOTES:	

NAME:	
SITE ADDRESS:	
USERNAME:	
PASSWORD:	
NOTES:	

NAME:	
SITE ADDRESS:	
USERNAME:	
PASSWORD:	
NOTES:	

NAME:	
SITE ADDRESS:	
USERNAME:	
PASSWORD:	
NOTES:	

NAME:	
SITE ADDRESS:	
USERNAME:	
PASSWORD:	
NOTES:	

NAME:	
SITE ADDRESS:	
USERNAME:	
PASSWORD:	
NOTES:	

NAME:	
SITE ADDRESS:	
USERNAME:	
PASSWORD:	
NOTES:	

NAME:	
SITE ADDRESS:	
USERNAME:	
PASSWORD:	
NOTES:	

NAME:	
SITE ADDRESS:	
USERNAME:	
PASSWORD:	
NOTES:	

NAME:	
SITE ADDRESS:	
USERNAME:	
PASSWORD:	
NOTES:	

NAME:	
SITE ADDRESS:	
USERNAME:	
PASSWORD:	
NOTES:	

NAME:	
SITE ADDRESS:	
USERNAME:	
PASSWORD:	
NOTES:	

NAME:	
SITE ADDRESS:	
USERNAME:	
PASSWORD:	
NOTES:	

NAME:	
SITE ADDRESS:	
USERNAME:	
PASSWORD:	
NOTES:	

NAME:	
SITE ADDRESS:	
USERNAME:	
PASSWORD:	
NOTES:	

NAME:	
SITE ADDRESS:	
USERNAME:	
PASSWORD:	
NOTES:	

NAME:	
SITE ADDRESS:	
USERNAME:	
PASSWORD:	
NOTES:	

NAME:	
SITE ADDRESS:	
USERNAME:	
PASSWORD:	
NOTES:	

NAME:	
SITE ADDRESS:	
USERNAME:	
PASSWORD:	
NOTES:	

NAME:	
SITE ADDRESS:	
USERNAME:	
PASSWORD:	
NOTES:	

NAME:	
SITE ADDRESS:	
USERNAME:	
PASSWORD:	
NOTES:	

NAME:	
SITE ADDRESS:	
USERNAME:	
PASSWORD:	
NOTES:	

NAME:	
SITE ADDRESS:	
USERNAME:	
PASSWORD:	
NOTES:	

NAME:	
SITE ADDRESS:	
USERNAME:	
PASSWORD:	
NOTES:	

NAME:	
SITE ADDRESS:	
USERNAME:	
PASSWORD:	
NOTES:	

NAME:	
SITE ADDRESS:	
USERNAME:	
PASSWORD:	
NOTES:	

NAME:	
SITE ADDRESS:	
USERNAME:	
PASSWORD:	
NOTES:	

NAME:	
SITE ADDRESS:	
USERNAME:	
PASSWORD:	
NOTES:	

NAME:	
SITE ADDRESS:	
USERNAME:	
PASSWORD:	
NOTES:	

NAME:	
SITE ADDRESS:	
USERNAME:	
PASSWORD:	
NOTES:	

NAME:	
SITE ADDRESS:	
USERNAME:	
PASSWORD:	
NOTES:	

NAME:	
SITE ADDRESS:	
USERNAME:	
PASSWORD:	
NOTES:	

NAME:	
SITE ADDRESS:	
USERNAME:	
PASSWORD:	
NOTES:	

NAME:	
SITE ADDRESS:	
USERNAME:	
PASSWORD:	
NOTES:	

NAME:	
SITE ADDRESS:	
USERNAME:	
PASSWORD:	
NOTES:	

NAME:	
SITE ADDRESS:	
USERNAME:	
PASSWORD:	
NOTES:	

NAME:	
SITE ADDRESS:	
USERNAME:	
PASSWORD:	
NOTES:	

NAME:	
SITE ADDRESS:	
USERNAME:	
PASSWORD:	
NOTES:	

NAME:	
SITE ADDRESS:	
USERNAME:	
PASSWORD:	
NOTES:	

NAME:	
SITE ADDRESS:	
USERNAME:	
PASSWORD:	
NOTES:	

NAME:	
SITE ADDRESS:	
USERNAME:	
PASSWORD:	
NOTES:	

NAME:	
SITE ADDRESS:	
USERNAME:	
PASSWORD:	
NOTES:	

NAME:	
SITE ADDRESS:	
USERNAME:	
PASSWORD:	
NOTES:	

NAME:	
SITE ADDRESS:	
USERNAME:	
PASSWORD:	
NOTES:	

NAME:	
SITE ADDRESS:	
USERNAME:	
PASSWORD:	
NOTES:	

NAME:	
SITE ADDRESS:	
USERNAME:	
PASSWORD:	
NOTES:	

NAME:	
SITE ADDRESS:	
USERNAME:	
PASSWORD:	
NOTES:	

NAME:	
SITE ADDRESS:	
USERNAME:	
PASSWORD:	
NOTES:	

NAME:	
SITE ADDRESS:	
USERNAME:	
PASSWORD:	
NOTES:	

NAME:	
SITE ADDRESS:	
USERNAME:	
PASSWORD:	
NOTES:	

NAME:	
SITE ADDRESS:	
USERNAME:	
PASSWORD:	
NOTES:	

NAME:	
SITE ADDRESS:	
USERNAME:	
PASSWORD:	
NOTES:	

NAME:	
SITE ADDRESS:	
USERNAME:	
PASSWORD:	
NOTES:	

NAME:	
SITE ADDRESS:	
USERNAME:	
PASSWORD:	
NOTES:	

NAME:	
SITE ADDRESS:	
USERNAME:	
PASSWORD:	
NOTES:	

NAME:	
SITE ADDRESS:	
USERNAME:	
PASSWORD:	
NOTES:	

NAME:	
SITE ADDRESS:	
USERNAME:	
PASSWORD:	
NOTES:	

NAME:	
SITE ADDRESS:	
USERNAME:	
PASSWORD:	
NOTES:	

NAME:	
SITE ADDRESS:	
USERNAME:	
PASSWORD:	
NOTES:	

NAME:	
SITE ADDRESS:	
USERNAME:	
PASSWORD:	
NOTES:	

NAME:	
SITE ADDRESS:	
USERNAME:	
PASSWORD:	
NOTES:	

NAME:	
SITE ADDRESS:	
USERNAME:	
PASSWORD:	
NOTES:	

NAME:	
SITE ADDRESS:	
USERNAME:	
PASSWORD:	
NOTES:	

NAME:	
SITE ADDRESS:	
USERNAME:	
PASSWORD:	
NOTES:	

NAME:	
SITE ADDRESS:	
USERNAME:	
PASSWORD:	
NOTES:	

NAME:	
SITE ADDRESS:	
USERNAME:	
PASSWORD:	
NOTES:	

NAME:	
SITE ADDRESS:	
USERNAME:	
PASSWORD:	
NOTES:	

NAME:	
SITE ADDRESS:	
USERNAME:	
PASSWORD:	
NOTES:	

NAME:	
SITE ADDRESS:	
USERNAME:	
PASSWORD:	
NOTES:	

NAME:	
SITE ADDRESS:	
USERNAME:	
PASSWORD:	
NOTES:	

NAME:	
SITE ADDRESS:	
USERNAME:	
PASSWORD:	
NOTES:	

NAME:	
SITE ADDRESS:	
USERNAME:	
PASSWORD:	
NOTES:	

NAME:	
SITE ADDRESS:	
USERNAME:	
PASSWORD:	
NOTES:	

NAME:	
SITE ADDRESS:	
USERNAME:	
PASSWORD:	
NOTES: